How I Met My Spouse

Heartwarming memories from the readers of Reminisce.

Editor
Mike Beno

Associate Editor
Sally Manich

Art Director
Julie Wagner

Production
Kristine Krueger

Photo Coordination
Trudi Bellin

Editorial Assistants
Blanche Comiskey, Joe Kertzman

International Standard Book Number 0-89821-115-8

Cover Photo: Ewing Galloway   **Back Cover Photo:** Jan S. Doward

4

Love Was Their Language

DURING World War II, I was a 19-year-old country girl living in the northeast of France.

My family struggled through 4 long years of Nazi occupation…we'd been bombed and we were cold and hungry through the long winter months of 1944.

When liberation finally came the next September, everyone was in a state of bliss.

To show our gratitude to the American liberators, all the village folks organized a little dance in their honor.

That was where I met my GI Joe. He was part of an American evacuation hospital set up in a field outside of my village.

Most girls in my age group didn't know much about dancing because all dances had been stopped during the occupation. Joe, on the other hand, was (and still is at age 75) a super dancer. In turn, he invited all the girls onto the dance floor for a whirl.

As it turned out, I was the only one who could follow his fancy footwork. (Being part of a dance-loving family, I'd been taught how to dance at home.)

Language Barrier No Problem

We danced the evening away not uttering a single word—he didn't speak any French and I didn't speak English.

Joe and I met again at subsequent dances. He had a friendly nature and soon started visiting my family. Even though hand gestures were the only means of communication, he won everybody's heart—including mine.

In November, the Allied army advanced through the mountains into Germany and the evacuation hospital followed. I assumed that was the end of our sign-language romance. How little I knew!

At Christmastime, enjoying a 3-day pass, he visited us again! By then he'd learned enough French to ask me to marry him. As odd as it may seem, I accepted.

For a while we were drowning in red tape—letters had to be written, interpreters sought. But finally all went well and the marriage authorizations came through.

We didn't see each other again until our wedding the following August. After a brief honeymoon, Joe returned to Germany where he was stationed. A while later he was sent stateside and discharged. The war was over.

We were reunited the following May when I sailed for New York City on a ship of European war brides. I still didn't know any English, and I was afraid I wouldn't recognize him without his Army uniform—but I did.

I learned the language quickly, and today, we're happily married and still dancing.   —*Theresa Comito, South Beach, New York*

They Had One Hot Romance!

I MET MY future spouse at a fire!

My folks and I were eating supper one night when my mother went into the kitchen to get my father another dish of stew. She passed a stairway, and noticed fire in a room upstairs! It was a bitter-cold night, 10° below zero.

A young man on his way home from work saw flames shooting out from our roof, and he banged on the door to make sure we knew. We had just called the fire department.

He immediately started helping us remove whatever we could from the house. Soon the smoke got so bad we couldn't save anything more, and we evacuated the house.

The wind was blowing on that below-zero night, and I wasn't wearing a coat—just a dress and shoes. I was very cold, and the young man told me to sit in his car and warm up. I refused, knowing that my family would be looking for me, and maybe think I was still in the burning house.

When he couldn't be of any more help he went on his way, but I recall thinking what a nice fellow he was. I saw him around town after that, but he never asked me out until the following spring.

We hit it off immediately, and by September, we were married. Our love has burned brightly and kept us warm through 47 years since.

—Ora Byron, Troy, Maine

Humorous Meeting Cracked Them Up

MY GRANDFATHER wrote his memoirs for his children and grandchildren when he was in his late 70s.

As a young man around the turn of the century, he went to New Castle, Wyoming and took a job at a grocery store. During his first week he spotted my grandmother on the street and said hello. This story of how they later met is an excerpt from Grandfather's memoirs:

"One day the store received a call for 2 dozen eggs to be delivered to a residence just a block from the store. It was a rush order and the delivery wagon was out on another call. So, I rolled up my apron, picked up the eggs and made the delivery on foot.

"I arrived at the house and knocked on the front door. It opened immediately—as if someone inside were waiting for me to bring those eggs.

"As I looked up, I stared into the eyes of the girl I had said hello to on the sidewalk several days earlier. In a sweet voice she asked, 'Won't you come in?'

"In answer to her invitation, I tried to step over the threshold, but I caught one toe on the top doorstep and fell flat on my face with the sack of eggs underneath me! Half of them broke and the front of me looked like scrambled eggs!

"The young lady was so convulsed with laughter that she was lying face down on the lounge with her left hand dangling over the side.

Was He Embarrassed!

"I saw that I was on the spot and would have to do a little clowning, so I walked over to the lounge, took her hand and, in a voice so low I almost choked, said, 'Don't worry, honey, we'll scrape the eggs off my chest and have an omelet together.'

"As I said that, I noticed an engagement ring on her finger and backed off, with an apology for calling her 'honey'. (I learned later she was engaged to a young law student living in Sheridan, Wyoming.)

"But then she arose from the couch, took the ring off her finger and laid it on the mantel above the fireplace. In a suddenly serious voice she told me her name, and asked for mine.

"She then said that the engagement ring was off her finger and would stay off until replaced by someone she could really love. She further explained that I had done something to her heart from the moment of our first sidewalk meeting. She said she often wondered when we would meet again.

"When she heard that I was clerking in the grocery store, she and her mother came up with plan to allow us to meet. After that delivery day, a courtship was started that lasted over a year.

"On the 17th day of August 1904, we were married."

—*Barbara Emeny, Idabel, Oklahoma*

A Pitcher's Proposals

DURING THE '40s, I worked as a secretary for Bill Veeck's old American Association Baseball Club, the Milwaukee Brewers. Charlie Grimm was the manager.

Most single men seemed to be in the service in 1943, but that year, a good-looking young man came from Iowa to pitch for the Brewers. He was shy and didn't hang out with the other guys. Instead, he spent quite a lot of his free time standing around in the office, just watching me work.

Early in that '43 season, he was sent to a farm club in Portsmouth, Virginia. I felt sorry for him because he was so shy and looked lonesome. I asked Charlie Grimm if he thought it would be okay if I wrote to this young man. That was a pretty bold move for a lady in those days!

Charlie asked the young man and he said sure, so we started corresponding.

Only a month went by and I got a marriage proposal by mail! My first reaction was to cool his heels, and in my next letter, I told him that we didn't even know each other and we should just be friends.

In September, when the season ended, he headed back home to Iowa. On the way, he stopped in Milwaukee and proposed to me again! This time, I accepted.

He went back to Iowa, and it took this shy boy a whole week to tell his folks he was "going back to Milwaukee to get married"!

In November, I married Vern in a small church wedding. We only had about 20 people there...including Charlie Grimm and Bill Veeck. That small ceremony led to a lifetime of love.   —*Vivian Nelson, Sun City, Arizona*

She's Not Lion, They Met at the Zoo!

MANY TEENS sought summer jobs at the almost-new Chicago Zoological Park (Brookfield Zoo) in the summer of 1936. At age 15, I was one of them.

I got a job working at a refreshment stand, and met quite a number of young co-workers that summer.

Some evenings when the zoo closed, we'd get together as a group to go on moonlight cruises on Lake Michigan, go horseback riding or stop to visit nearby Riverview amusement park.

One Sunday while I was working at the refreshment stand, the man who drove the ice cream truck said to me, "Phyllie, don't go to those shindigs with any of these guys...do I have a nice fella for you!"

Later, he introduced me to Vern, his helper.

We were both 15 and I was not allowed to date unless with a group of kids. Vern and I did manage to get on the two-seater rides at Riverview, dance a couple times on the cruises and ride together on moonlight horseback outings with the group.

But, because of my strict upbringing and the fact that we lived a few towns apart, ours was at first a summers-only romance. Later, Vern called my parents and got permission to take me to his high school's homecoming game and dance.

From then on we were allowed only one date a week until Christmas 1940, when we became engaged. Then we were allowed two dates—one of which was on Sundays with the family.

Vern was only 20, so his mother had to go with us to the courthouse to get our marriage license. We shyly gave our names to the clerk. In a very loud voice, and much to our embarrassment, Vern's mother boomed, "That's spelled V-E-R-N-A-R-D! Not Vern!" She was correct, of course, but both of our faces were vermilion.

On August 8, 1941, we were married in my parents' home. I'll never forget walking down the staircase to recordings of the Andrews Sisters singing *I'll Be With You in Apple Blossom Time* and *Because* by Deanna Durbin.

—*Phyllis Miller, Nevada City, California*

He Harvested More Than Tomatoes

I WAS A recent widower and I had a 3-year-old son to raise. My mother, who was in her 80s at the time, insisted that I move in with her. Reluctantly, I sold my house and moved back with Mom.

I always liked to putter in the garden, so I soon planted some tomatoes in a small section in the backyard next to the fence.

One day my little son came running inside crying and pointing out the door. All he could say was, "That lady! That lady!" I went out to the backyard to see what the fuss was about.

Lady Turned Out to Be Neighbor

"That lady" turned out to be our neighbor, who was standing by my tomatoes with a smile on her face. When I asked her what the trouble was, she said she told my son that anything hanging over the fence was hers!

I immediately hung my body over the fence! She laughed heartily, and not too long after that, we were engaged and married.

It's been 25 years since then, and I still plant tomatoes every spring. When I do, my mind always wanders back to that day when I hung my body over the fence.

Come to think of it, those were the best tomatoes I ever grew!

—*Fred Buecher, Hazelwood, Missouri*

Tale of a Trash Can

I MET MY HUSBAND in a trash can!

It all began during World War II. I was working in a defense plant in Los Angeles, and there were so many soldiers, sailors and Marines on the West Coast at that time, that it was impossible not to meet some of them.

I went on a date with one Marine, who was soon to ship overseas. He asked for my picture, and I obliged, writing my address on the back for future correspondence.

Apparently, he didn't see much future in a relationship with me, because he threw my picture in the trash! My future husband, also a Marine, happened by that trash can and spotted my picture. He fished it out and began writing to me.

NOBLE GESTURE? Young Marine Jim Noble found future wife's discarded photo in garbage can! He wrote Nancy, set up the 1945 meeting at right, and they married a short time later. Recent photo above proves this story ended "picture perfect".

In his first letter he introduced himself, Jim Noble, and mentioned that his hometown was Cicero, Indiana. Since the lead man at my defense plant also hailed from Cicero, I asked him one day if he happened to know this Jim Noble fellow.

Had Him in Suspense

"I sure do!" he said. "I'll tell you everything about him and his family so that when you write back he'll wonder how in the world you know everything about him!"

Well, when I received my second letter from Jim, he was practically on his knees begging to know how I knew so much about him and his family. Eventually, I fessed up.

Two months later, the war ended. Jim came to Los Angeles and called me for a date. We met downtown on the corner of 7th and Broadway, and I was so excited to see this tall good-looking Marine striding down the block to meet me. Little did I then know that this handsome Marine and I would be married in a matter of 2 weeks!

Today, all I can say is "Thank you, I don't recall your name, for throwing my picture in that trash can so many miles away, so many years ago. You did me a favor that day…my life has been *great* ever since!"

—*Nancy Noble, Vancouver, Washington*

She Had Help in Winning Hero's Heart

MY HERO was a boy in my high school class. He didn't know I existed, and I had been trying in vain to get him to notice me.

I knew he had to walk past my house to get home from school, so one day I devised a plan. I rushed home after school and called for "Betty", our Irish terrier. I grabbed Betty's leash and off we went for a "chance" meeting with Mr. Right.

As my hero passed my house, Betty and I were calmly walking along toward him. He and I stopped, exchanged greetings, and talked about school and dogs. Each day as my hero passed our house, Betty and I just happened to be out there, and soon, the conversations turned to more personal things—like dating!

Now, 36 years later, my hero-husband and I still love dogs. But I did have to confess to him that the only times I ever walked Betty were those days when that little co-conspirator helped me capture his heart!

—*Paula Crookshank, Hohenwald, Tennessee*

It Was a Ball to Meet His Sweetheart

IN THE SUMMER of 1942, I was going through basic training in Texas. One of my buddies, Paul, was a recruit from Chicago.

Basics were almost over, and Paul was scheduled to attend officer's training. I was about to be shipped to another duty station, and neither of us had any idea where we'd be sent.

As the truck carrying me and some other recruits was about to leave, Paul came running out of the recreation hall where he'd been playing Ping-Pong. He asked for my new address and I told him I didn't know it.

Quickly, he scribbled something on the Ping-Pong ball he was holding. Then, running alongside the moving truck, he threw me the ball. I tucked it into my jacket pocket and we rolled off into the vastness of West Texas.

Two months passed at my new base, and during a surprise inspection I received a demerit for having a foreign object in my jacket pocket. Investigation produced an offending Ping-Pong ball, which I'd completely forgotten about!

Paul's smudged writing showed his home address in Chicago, as well as the names of his two sisters. Now I could get in touch with my buddy!

I wrote to the girls asking for Paul's new address, and his younger sister, Jennie, answered me. As time went on, we wrote back and forth.

Well, I never did write to Paul. The next time I saw my old buddy was after the war, when Jennie and I were married and expecting our first child.

Jennie and I have now enjoyed many wonderful years together...and Paul's still my friend! —*B.E. Chitwood, Crowley, Texas*

She Didn't Scare Him Off

IN NOVEMBER of 1941, a friend told me her brother was coming home from the Army for Thanksgiving. I laughingly told her, "Tell him there's a girl here who's cross-eyed, knock-kneed and pigeon-toed and she'd like to meet him."

I was just kidding, of course, and soon forgot about my little joke. But on Thanksgiving, my friend brought her brother over to meet me, saying he wanted to see what a girl with all those problems actually looked like!

Between Thanksgiving and Christmas he visited me often and we became acquainted. When he went back to the service, he wrote me often, and by March we were engaged.

He wasn't scared off when he first heard about me, and he hasn't been since—we were married in July 1942. —*Mary Heinlein*
Hot Springs, Arkansas

Whirlwind Courtship
'Raised Some Dust'

I WAS AN 18-year-old civilian truck driver for the military gunnery school in my hometown of Las Vegas in November 1944. It was an unusual job for a girl, but there was a war on!

I drove everything from a scooter to a 2-ton turret truck, but I mostly drove a little pickup for the base plumber. I'd drive him to his jobs and sit in my truck until he finished.

One day as I was waiting behind one of the mess halls, a military truck raced up behind me, raising a cloud of dust and gravel. The GI driver slammed on his brakes, jumped out of his truck and came running up to

13

me. I was wondering what in the world I could have done wrong!

"Are you married?" he asked.

"No!" I replied.

He said his name was Joe, he was from Kingston, New York and he was happy to meet me. With that, he drove off.

Well, the next day the same thing happened. Only this time after slamming on his brakes and rushing over to me he asked, "Will you marry me?" I laughed and said, "I'll think about it and let you know when the war's over!"

That night I told my folks about this crazy soldier from New York who asked me to marry him. We all laughed and thought it was pretty funny!

Joe asked me out, and we went to a couple of movies during the next month. I invited him to our home for Christmas dinner, and he spent New Year's weekend with us.

The following Monday he once again came running up to my parked pickup. "Let's get married on Saturday!" he said.

This time, I agreed...and my parents exploded!

I was 19, Joe was 21, and we'd only know each other 6 weeks. They said he was a nice guy, but we should wait until we knew each other better, or at least until after the war. But it seemed like everybody was in a hurry during the war.

We have celebrated numerous wedding anniversaries since. We have three children, 12 grandchildren and six great-grandchildren. So, despite what we were told, some short acquaintances do become long and happy relationships!
                                        —*Phyllis Ferrara, Forest Grove, Oregon*

They Sang for Their Supper

SHORTLY AFTER I began teaching at an academy in Maine, I accepted an invitation from the headmaster and his wife to attend a Kiwanis Club supper. When we arrived I discovered it was a "box supper", and a "box" had been prepared in my name.

Box suppers were popular in those days. For these events, young ladies would prepare a meal for two and pack it in box. Later, all the young men would bid on the boxes without knowing who prepared it or what was inside.

The highest bidder won the supper, and got to share it with the lady who prepared the meal.

I was never keen on blind dates, so I wasn't too happy about sitting down to supper with a stranger. But the fellow who bought the box with my

MEN IN UNIFORM were stationed all around the country during WWII—making for some interesting meetings.

Ewing Galloway

name on it seemed presentable. He was well-dressed, had a nice speaking voice and appeared as shy about the whole thing as I felt.

Later in the evening, the Kiwanians had their customary sing-along. Being musical, I joined in heartily, only to notice, right beside me, the most beautiful bass singing voice I'd ever heard! Suddenly, my shyness was gone and my date seemed to relax, too.

Within a month we had our first real date, and we later married. Through the years we've spent many wonderful hours in song.

—*Daphne Merrill, Auburn, Maine*

He 'Caught Her' at Home Plate

I MET MY SPOUSE in college, at an old-fashioned softball game.

When I got up to bat, I hit a triple. The next batter hit the ball, so I started running toward home. The ball was thrown to the catcher who quickly decided that, girl or no girl, he had to tag me out. We collided at home plate!

At 125 pounds, I was no match for that 195-pound catcher, and I found myself flat on the ground. Later that year, I fell for him in another way— that catcher became my husband!
—*Candy Feathers*
Bell Buckle, Tennessee

She Spied on Her Guy

SHORTLY after I began my sophomore year at West Geauga High School in Chesterland, Ohio, I noticed a "new boy" in school. He was an upperclassman who had moved to our little town from Cleveland. My new goal in life became keeping track of his every move!

I quickly set up a spy system with my friends, and was given reports several times each day as to what HE was wearing, who HE was talking to and where HE was.

Since I received conflicting reports on what his name was, I dubbed him "the boy with the eyes" because he had the most beautiful blue eyes I'd ever seen.

For weeks I peeked around corners to catch glimpses of him. I'd pick just the right table in the cafeteria (close enough to watch him, but not close enough for him to see me watching). Whenever he looked my way, I'd giggle and hide behind my friends. It didn't take him long to figure something was up, and soon, he seemed to be watching me!

Then came the fateful day—the blizzard of '61. The snowstorm had hit so suddenly that all the school buses were delayed.

I was standing outside waiting for the bus with my friends when someone said, "HE's looking at you!" Everyone in the group began giggling, and when they saw him start to walk our way, they scattered in all directions. Like the cheese—I stood alone!

"The boy with the eyes" walked right up to me and said, "Hi...can I have your phone number?"

Snow might have been piling up all around us, but I felt like I was melting as I watched him write my phone number on the cover of a matchbook.

To this day, I'm thankful that Mother Nature had a temper tantrum back in '61. That storm brought us together...forever!　　　—*Candi Toth*
York, Pennsylvania

They Won Their Prizes at the Fair

I MET MY loving wife on a crisp fall day in 1956.

I'd gone to the station to catch a bus for New York to see another girl I'd been dating. The county fair was going on near the station, and since I had a couple hours to kill before my bus left, I decided to walk around the fairgrounds.

I ran into my best friend's sister, who was enjoying the fair with two other girls. She introduced me to her friends, one of whom was a cute brunette who seemed a little shy. I asked her if she'd like to go on any of the rides, and after a little coaxing from my friend's sister, she said yes.

While we were riding the "octopus", some of my friends spotted us and dared me to kiss her—which I did.

Everybody cheered and clapped, and the shy young lady blushed. Then she surprised me by saying, "If they thought that was a kiss, watch *this!*"

You may have already guessed that I never did take that bus to New York. We were married the following year.

All these years later, we still love going to the fair. She likes to say she got the "booby prize", but she's only kidding. I say I got the grand prize.

—Edwin Hill, Santa Barbara, California

A 'Match' Made in Texas

OUR NEIGHBOR was in charge of the USO in my hometown of Slaton, Texas. One day in the summer of 1943, she asked if my younger sisters and I could help serve refreshments to the boys that would be passing through on troop trains.

My sisters and I pulled a "Red Flyer" coaster wagon full of Coca-Colas up and down the station platform, passing them to the GIs who were reaching through the windows of the train.

One fellow asked me for my address and I said, "No, I don't give my address to strangers", and we continued passing out Cokes.

When our task was done, we walked back past the troops to the station. The same GI said, "Won't you please write your name and address on this matchbook? I promise to write and tell you all about the South Pacific."

I figured there was no harm in his writing me, so I jotted my address on the matchbook and tossed it back to him. About a dozen other GIs grabbed for it—but the "begging GI" managed to catch it.

From then on, he wrote almost every day. Five months later, on January 29, 1944, he came home on a pass and gave me an engagement ring. Five months after that, he sent me a train ticket to Camp Wheeler, Georgia, where we were married in June of 1944.

We've had great years together, and I'm glad to this day that he persuaded me to write my address on that matchbook!
—Betty Swartz
Sun City, Arizona

WINNING COUPLE. Rodeo riders Don and Joan Lutz teamed up to ride in competition in '45. By '49, they'd won plenty of awards (top). They were married in 1950 (at left), and today their son, Donnie, and daughter, Marty Jo, continue work on the rodeo and horse show circuit.

Rodeo Riders Wed on Horseback

MY HUSBAND and I met at a horse show in 1945, and after we'd gotten to know one another, it didn't take much "horse sense" to see we'd fallen in love!

Don was 15 and I was 13 when we met, and he asked me to compete as his partner in a "rescue race". Since I'd been riding competitively since I was 8, I was more than willing to join him. We ended up taking third place.

We rode together for the next 5 years, winning our share of trophies and ribbons. We began dating, too. Finally, in 1950, we were married on horseback at a rodeo held in Lewisburg, Ohio. (See photos at left.)

The minister rode in a buggy, and all the attendants were on horseback. The ceremony was performed under an arch decorated with pink and white crepe paper. Over 2,500 people attended our wedding!

Through the years our love has grown—as has our love for horses! We've run a Western store and riding school since 1959. After 5,000 students, our business is still going strong…as is our wonderful marriage!

—*Joan Lutz, Eaton, Ohio*

Round the Rink to Romance

IN 1927, I lived on a stock farm in Texas and hardly ever got to go to town to see how other people lived. I kept hearing about the fun people were having in a little town of Clyde, Texas, where they had brought in a portable roller skating rink.

I wanted to try skating for myself. Once on the rink, though, I spent more time on the floor than on my feet.

A very cute blond girl about 15 years old saw I was having a lot of trouble standing up in skates. She took delight in skating into me and knocking me down!

One particular time I was holding onto the rail trying to get enough nerve to try it again. She came by and stopped. I was very angry at her and told her that she was a smart aleck!

When I asked her why she kept knocking me down, she skated off and called over her shoulder, "Because it's fun!"

She made two or three rounds and I was still holding onto the rail. I called her over and told her I would get even with her if I had to marry her to do it! After a few more nights at the rink, I asked her for our first date.

This was at the beginning of the Depression, and there were times when

I didn't have the money to take her out. She and I and two or three other couples would go horseback riding. As time went on, we fell madly in love. I gave her the best horse on the ranch.

Then we had a lover's quarrel and broke up. I wanted my horse back, but she said, "Never—not on your life." I told her that I would get my horse back if I had to make up with her and get married to do it.

And I did. We were married on August 9, 1930. I made good on two promises that day...and got my horse back to boot! —*Winford Kelly*
Stoutland, Missouri

Love Blossomed Below Deck

I MET MY HUSBAND under water!

While working as a hostess at a Navy Mother's Club, I was invited to an open house on one of the ships. The tour was being held in celebration of "Navy Day" (October 27).

While touring the engine room (which is below the water level), I was introduced to a charming young sailor.

Every weekend after that, he rode the bus some 100 miles to visit me, until he shipped out again. We corresponded for the long months he spent at sea, and the following "Navy Day", exactly a year later, we were married!

We just celebrated 45 years of marriage, and I still remember how we met under water! —*Audrey Surma, Richmond, Virginia*

Amusement Ride Was Their 'Wheel of Fortune'

THE CALIFORNIA STATE FAIR is traditionally held on Labor Day weekend—one of the hottest times of the year. But on that weekend in 1954, it was downright chilly.

My sister and I stepped into an Air Force exhibit tent just to warm up. A young sergeant who was manning one of the displays asked me if I'd like a ride on the Ferris wheel. I wanted to, but it was just too cold! He solved the problem by lending me his sweater.

We've been going around together ever since! We were married just 3 months after we took that Ferris wheel ride. I still have that sweater…and him, too! *—Mary Rogers, El Dorado Hills, California*

Ravishing Redhead
Skated into His Life

I FIRST saw Mary in August of 1925.

My Navy buddies and I were relaxing at a roller skating rink, when the most beautiful redhead I'd ever seen skated up to us.

Well, maybe "skated" isn't the word. Out of control and groping for the hand rails, she actually fell right at my feet!

I quickly came to her aid and we had two dates before my ship sailed. We were separated for a whole year but continued our courtship through correspondence. We were married shortly after my ship returned.

It's been many years since Mary skated into my life, and for almost all of them, she's been my wife! *—Eddie Wishman, Colorado Springs, Colorado*

Romance Bloomed
'100 Miles from Nowhere'

I WAS IN HIGH SCHOOL during World War II. Most of the young men in our small town were drafted, including our music teacher.

During my senior year, a young man right out of college came to replace our music teacher. Young Mr. Bailey wasn't excited about landing a teaching job in "a little town 100 miles from nowhere", and at first, I didn't like him much.

Right before senior prom, my boyfriend and I had a falling out. I was heartsick when prom day arrived. But Mr. Bailey showed up at my door with a lovely corsage that matched his beautiful blue eyes. I cried on his shoulder as he consoled me about my broken date.

When the school year ended, instead of going back home, Mr. Bailey took a job with the telephone company where I was an operator. We began dating after that, and when he proposed, I was still calling him Mr. Bailey. (Old habits are hard to break!)

It wasn't long before Uncle Sam called him, too, so we hurriedly made

SERVICEMAN'S KISS remains in the memory of Jean Peters, who first kissed her favorite soldier in 1943 (see her story).

NEW

RAILWAY

Archive Photos/Lambert

our wedding plans. We were married in a week and he left 12 days later.

It's now several decades, three children and six grandchildren later, but Mr. Bailey and I are still happily married. And he never did leave that "little town 100 miles from nowhere". *—Mrs. Lawrence Bailey*
Shinglehouse, Pennsylvania

❤ ❤ ❤

'Good-Bye' Was Really 'Hello'

IN OCTOBER 1943, I was working at the State Capitol in Pierre, South Dakota. When a small Air Force base was built outside town, we girls were delighted. There were very few eligible men in Pierre, and lots of girls worked at the capitol!

One night the Provost Marshall at the base called and asked if we could round up everyone we knew and get a good crowd together at the train station. At midnight, the first group of men from the base was shipping overseas. We were to gather for moral support and say some good-byes.

My co-workers and I called everyone we could think of, and when we got to the train station, there were people everywhere. As I walked in the station, a friend said, "Jean, this is Pete", and he walked off.

Pete and I were just awkwardly standing there making small talk, when I noticed that everyone was kissing some serviceman good-bye—except me!

Pete was handy, so I leaned over, kissed him and airily said, "Bye!"

He looked at me very seriously and said, "But I'm not going anywhere! I just got here today—I'm a replacement!" Boy, was I embarrassed!

We dated for 3 months and then were married. So you truly could say that little kiss of mine really started something big! *—Jean Peters*
Evansville, Indiana

❤ ❤ ❤

They Were 'Berry' Happy to Meet

ONE OF MY JOYS in life after being widowed for several years was making strawberry jam for my son and son-in-law for Father's Day.

One June day I was spending a long time at the fruit market, picking just the right berries for my jam.

Suddenly I heard a voice behind me, and it was a gentleman wondering out loud how you go about cleaning strawberries. His wife used to handle that kitchen task, but he had been a widower for quite some time.

I didn't bother to look up but just remarked on how the job should be done. Then I apologized for taking so long at the fruit counter and moved along.

Later, as I walked to the end of the aisle, that same gentleman was standing there waiting for me. He introduced himself and thanked me for my help.

He then invited me for coffee, and he was so charming that I accepted his invitation. Coffee led to weekend brunch, and, 7 months later, to marriage.

Our wedding cake was strawberry-flavored and we often shared a secret smile when that sweet summer fruit was mentioned. —*Mary Ann Fritch Lansing, Michigan*

Their Relationship 'Developed'

WHILE ENTERING a dark room to develop some X-rays during my senior year of dental school—with my eyes unaccustomed to the dark—I bumped into something soft that smelled lovely.

It was a young lady who was studying to become a hygienist. I was too startled and shy to ask her name at the time, so I had to find out later. Eventually, I talked with her, and arranged a meeting at the school library.

Two years after that chance encounter, we started a marriage that is now in its 53rd year. So what once started in the dark had a very bright future! —*Henry Junemann, Santa Rosa, California*

Secret Admirer Popped the Question On the Night This Couple Met

MY FUTURE HUSBAND and I were both in the service during World War II, stationed at Hammer Field in Fresno, California.

He told me he used to watch me walk down the flight line, and often followed me into the coffee shop.

He and a buddy would sit right behind me and a friend, and then proceed to eavesdrop on our conversations. So, by the time my spouse and I actually met, he knew nearly everything about me. He later told me that he remarked to his buddy, "Someday that little WAC is going to be my wife."

One night a WAC friend of mine suggested we go to a dance at the service club. I learned later that my future spouse had asked my friend to bring me there.

When we got to the dance I noticed that one guy kept yelling to the band to play *Twilight Time*. I thought to myself, I wish they'd play it so he'd just shut up!

When they played his song, he asked me to dance. After we danced a few times and talked for quite a while, he asked if he could walk me back to my barracks.

That night we stood in the rain and talked for hours. He told me he had loved me from afar for a long time and he wanted to marry me. I didn't know what to say because we had just met!

I really liked him a lot, but I thought what we were feeling couldn't be love...not this fast. Well, it turned out to be a case of love at first sight, because I accepted his proposal 2 days later.

Some people said it wouldn't last, but we proved them wrong...and we're still proving them wrong today! —*Wandine Kain, Richmond, Virginia*

A Cone for a Canine?

I WALKED my sister's dog every evening when I was a teenager. On our way back home we would stop at the malt shop, where the local teens would "hang out". I always bought myself an ice cream cone.

One night one of the boys bought an ice cream cone *for the dog*, then asked me if he could walk us both home!

I went with him for 2 years before we were married, 62 years ago.

—*Margaret Arneth, Beachwood, New Jersey*

The Magic's Still There

MY COLLEGE STUDIES had been interrupted by 3 years' worth of Air Force duty in World War II. But by January 1946, I was hitting the books once more.

Money was really tight, but I scraped up enough to buy a meal ticket at

USO DANCES provided a great place for couples to meet during the WWII years.

a local restaurant. A certain waitress worked there with a beautiful smile and boundless energy. I liked her, so, of course, I always gave her a hard time.

One morning she served me clam chowder for breakfast just to get even! She usually worked until midnight, and it wasn't long before she had me volunteering to sweep up so she could get off sooner.

She'd save her nickel and dime tips in a big piggy bank, and just to tease her, I'd pretend to drop a 50¢ piece in the slot, then palm the coin "magically". One night when I tried that trick, she grabbed the coin from my hand and put it in the bank. Then she challenged me to magically retrieve it.

Of course, I couldn't! Now, in those days, 50¢ could buy a whole meal, so with a sizable investment in this young lady, I had no choice but to propose.

Today, Bonnie and I have three children and two grandchildren...and the magic hasn't ever ended for us! —*Bill Harrison*
Fairfield Glade, Tennessee

Soldier Stole USO Girl's Heart

I LIVED in Vicksburg, Mississippi in 1945. During the war, our town was always filled with servicemen.

My sister Sybil and I were USO girls, so on Saturday evenings and Sunday afternoons we visited with servicemen at the USO.

One hot July afternoon I was chatting with some of these lonely boys, when I looked up and saw a tall, slender, handsome soldier coming through the door. Did my heart skip a beat!

Oh, if I could only meet that soldier, I thought, but it didn't happen. He was walking fast and went straight to the back of the room where he spoke with some other soldiers. Then he left...but I couldn't get the picture of him out of my mind.

Two weeks later at the USO, Sybil and I were visiting with a boy named Bill. Bill had a cast on his left leg, so he couldn't get around too well. He said to us, "My buddy has a car and I'll see if he'll drive us around the National Military Park today, if you'd care to go."

That sounded nice, so we met later on. When the car rolled up, *did my heart skip another beat*! Bill's buddy was the same soldier I'd been seeing in my dreams for the past 2 weeks.

Today, I find my husband just as exciting as I did that day years ago, when I first saw him walk into the USO. —*Louise Estes, Gardendale, Alabama*

'Good Boys Make Good Husbands'

I WORKED AS A NURSE in an intensive care unit, and one of my favorite patients was a wonderful woman with a devoted son who visited her daily. That son often called me to get updates on his mother's progress, and I was happy to provide the information.

Often, that sweet lady would share her worries with me about her single son. "My good boy, Gerry," she'd say, "why can't he find a nice wife like you?"

Several years later, I worked in the emergency room of another hospital and Gerry happened to be working there as a security guard.

Some nights were incredibly busy and I was always impressed at how he just pitched in and helped in whatever ways he could. Other nights seemed to drag on and on, so we had lots of time to talk and become acquainted.

Sadly, Gerry's mother passed away 1 year before we were married. But I'm sure that somewhere she's very pleased that her "good boy" got the wife she so often prayed for.
—*Mrs. Gerard Laferriere*
Knights Landing, California

Pup Fetched Her Heart

I WAS ON SUMMER BREAK from law school and working as a clerk in a Denver law firm. The work demanded long hours of research, so that left me precious little time to enjoy the Colorado sunshine.

On Sunday afternoons I'd try to catch some sun by bringing my law books to the park. One beautiful sunny Sunday I chanced to look up from my book to see a long-haired blond contemplating how to get through a pattern of lawn sprinklers without getting wet.

"Chicken!" I yelled, amused at her fear of a few drops of water on such a hot day. She looked up to see what sort of rude character would be so obnoxious.

It may have ended there, but I had a secret weapon with me, guaranteed to melt women's hearts. "Ingrid" was my almost unbearably cute elkhound puppy.

I told Ingrid to "sic her", pointing to the startled young woman. Ingrid, one of the brightest and friendliest animals you'd ever want to meet, obediently trotted up to Ann and begged to be followed.

Nothing Lassie or Rin Tin Tin ever did could exceed Ingrid's performance that day. Who could resist those big eyes and that tightly curled white flag of a tail?

Ann followed Ingrid right back to me. We exchanged names and discovered our birthdays were both August 30. We were married shortly after that...and I've never forgotten her birthday!　　　—*Charles Hillestad*
Denver Colorado

She Went from Reference to Romance

THE LIBRARY OF CONGRESS in Washington, D.C. isn't a likely place for romance, but that's where I met my husband.

I was an Army nurse stationed at Walter Reed Hospital during the Korean War. In the evenings I took a public-speaking course.

"Statehood for Hawaii" was the topic for my next class, so I went to the library to gather information. I stood for a long time in that huge place, not knowing where to start.

Finally, a young man came over and asked if he could help. I told him he sure could!

I got my information and gave my speech without a hitch. And that helpful young man has helped me in every way ever since!
　　　—*Dorothy Cutts, Huntsville, Alabama*

They Danced on a Dare

I WAS TEACHING at a little rural school in 1926. It was some distance from my home, so I boarded with a lady who owned a farm near school.

One year she hired several young men to work the farm. I was walking home from school one day when the young men dared one fellow in the group to ask the schoolteacher for a date.

He stepped out from the group and asked me to go to the dance with him that very night. I surprised them all by accepting! Many dates followed, and 6 months later, we were married.

Our marriage lasted 63 years, and I've always been glad my husband took that dare.　　　—*Leone Congdon, Mansfield, Pennsylvania*

No matter how prospective spouses met one another, their meeting led up to that big occasion that all happy young couples dream of—their wedding day. These wedding portraits from the good old days prove that, whether well off or poor, it made no difference...everyone looked their very best on this day of days.

Dolly Bruff of Belding, Michigan shared the handsome photo of her parents at left. The two Polish immigrants arrived in the U.S. in the late 1800s and were married in 1906. With little to live on and 16 children to raise, they worked hard to coax a living out of their Michigan farm.

Herman Derrer and his bride, Adelheid (below), went into their 1905 wedding day with a little more wherewithal behind them. Herman was a successful farmer with 200 acres of land when he and Adelheid set up housekeeping at his Iowa farm. This priceless photo was shared by the couple's grandniece, Vivian Hanawalt of Meservey, Iowa.

SURREY FLURRY. Aaron and Anna McDaniel (above) were wed in 1910. Daughter Janice Christian of Cypress, California says, "Mom was pouting because she was angry with Dad. He'd reserved a surrey with a fringe on top. When the stable owner gave the only fringed surrey to someone else, the men got into a fight!"

Sheet Music Was Sweet Music

AFTER GRADUATING from high school in 1931, I got a job in Ft. Worth, Texas. My office was on the third floor of a building that housed a music store on the ground floor.

Every morning as I walked past the store, I noticed a very good-looking young man busily working near the front window. He seemed to be watching me, too! We exchanged smiles on a regular basis and soon the smiles turned into waves.

I asked around and learned that his name was Earl. I finally mustered the courage to walk into the store and meet him. Though I wasn't the least bit musical, I asked if he had the sheet music for *Tumbling Tumbleweeds*.

He did! We started courting (in a rumble seat) and got married on February 4, 1933. After all these years of marriage, *Tumbleweeds* is still "our song"!
                                        —*Ophelia Waltrip, Midland, Texas*

It's Been Heavenly

ONE FRIDAY evening in 1940, our church youth group was having a dance. I attended with some other girls, thinking it would be just another jukebox dance. Two of the regular boys from our group brought a new fellow to the dance, and just as they entered, a "get-acquainted circle dance" began.

The new fellow joined in, took my hand and said, "I thought all the angels were in Heaven." What a line…but I fell for it!

Three years later, we were married. Our happy marriage produced five sons and a daughter and now we have 12 wonderful grandchildren. Time's passed, but it still feels like "heaven" to me!
                                        —*Mary Bellmore*
                                        Playa Del Rey, California

A Husband Was Her Real Reward

WHILE WALKING down the hall at school one day, I saw a wad of paper on the floor. I kicked it a couple of times and it came unfolded. It was three $20 bills! A tall, dark and very handsome young man, whom I had admired from afar, was walking a bit ahead of me. I rushed up to him and asked if he'd lost any money. He felt his pocket and said, "Yes! Sixty dollars!"

"Here," I said, and rushed off to class.

The next day when he saw me in a classroom, he walked in and asked me for a date. I happily accepted.

Many dates followed, and now, after 55 years, two sons, five grand-children and one great-grandchild, I'm pleased to say that the love I found back in high school made me a far richer person than that $60 ever could have.　　　　　　　　　　　—*Cleata Messer, Thomaston, Georgia*

Their Love Was a 'Shoe-in'

OURS WAS a true-to-life Cinderella story. During the '50s, it was a com-mon icebreaker at dances for all the young women to take off one shoe and put it in a pile in the center of the room. Each young man, in turn, would choose a shoe. Its owner would be his partner for the next dance.

On Halloween in 1958, my church youth group had a square dance, and we invited youth groups from two other churches. Since few people knew each other, the "shoe dance" was the perfect icebreaker.

I dutifully put my shoe in the pile and kept my eye on it. I watched as a tall young man walked to the jumble of shoes, and picked mine out of the pile. Without hesitation, he looked up—directly into my eyes.

It was the beginning of an enduring relationship. He's still my Prince Charming!　　　　　　　　　　　—*Joyce Deily, Charlottesville, Virginia*

They Took the Bus to Bliss

IT WAS Memorial Day weekend, 1954. I was taking the Greyhound bus from Seattle to Wenatchee, Washington to visit my aunt and uncle.

Waiting to board the bus, I spotted the most beautiful girl I'd ever seen. She was getting on the same bus!

We had to cross the mountains from Seattle to Wenatchee. At Bluet Pass we hit some road construction, and I could see "my girl" was getting a little carsick.

The driver stopped and had all of us get off to get some air. My first romantic words to this beautiful girl were, "You're not looking too good."

I found out her name was Dolores and she was on a weekend trip, too. When we boarded the bus, I made a point to sit behind her and we talked all the way to Wenatchee.

My aunt and uncle were there to meet me, and her friends were there for her. I hoped we'd take the same bus back to Seattle!

Monday evening came. My aunt and uncle took me to the Greyhound depot and I boarded the bus. Suddenly, I saw my dream girl getting out of a car with her suitcase! I jumped off the bus to give her a hand, and asked if I could sit with her on the way back. She accepted.

It was a very romantic ride on the "Hound". Moonlight shone on the snowcapped peaks through the crystal-clear mountain air. I held her hand and talked her into a little kiss.

On December 18, 1954, I married Dolores in Washington. Since then, I'm proud to say, she's been the "(Washington) apple of my eye"!
—*Guy Murren, Tunas, Missouri*

She Never Forgot His Smile

I FIRST laid eyes on my love in the corridor of St. Joseph School in 1936, while he was being scolded by Sister Veronica.

When I passed him in that hallway, I couldn't help but notice his dark curly hair and striking smile.

He wasn't aware I was watching, but I just knew that someday, somewhere, somehow, we would be together.

We grew up and went our separate ways, and it took 7 long years before I saw him again.

My cousin and I were walking down the street when I saw a cute sailor striding toward us. His white hat was cocked to one side, partially covering those black curls, and he flashed a brilliant smile that matched his hat.

It was HIM!

We had never actually met, but it turned out that my cousin knew him from school. She was happy to introduce me to that sailor, but I was so tongue-tied, all I could do was stutter and stammer.

Despite that, he asked me out, and we enjoyed several dates before the war separated us for a time. We wrote to one another faithfully, and when he asked me to wait for him I didn't hesitate.

Even today, he still calls me his bride. Somehow, I always knew that would happen!
—*Julia Kapinos, Norwich, Connecticut*

A WINNING SMILE can often lead to romance, as Julia Kapinos recalls in her story.

There Was 'Electricity' Between Them!

THOMAS EDISON was indirectly responsible for my meeting my future husband.

It was August of 1955, and I was working in an office in downtown Wabash, Indiana. Wabash was the first electrically lighted city in the world and we were celebrating the 75th anniversary of that event with the "Diamond Jubilee of Light".

My future spouse had a summer job working for the company that was in charge of decorating our town for the big celebration.

He came into our office to ask if we wanted the front of our building decorated. We sure did, so I was assigned to work with him on the decorations for a whole weekend. As we worked together, we became friends.

Sometime after the celebration, he went back to school at Indiana University. But we didn't forget one another! In fact, we were married 3 months later, on Thanksgiving Day.

I've always been thankful he came into my life, and I feel as if I can truly say, "Thank you, Thomas Edison!"
—Connie Motz
Terre Haute, Indiana

The Coldest Winter Warmed Their Hearts

THE WINTER of 1937 was bitterly cold in Iowa—often 20° below zero or colder. I was a salesman for a wholesale grocery company in a small town there.

Every morning before going out on the road, all the salesmen would gather for a pep talk from the boss. One morning our office girl came in during the end of the salesmen's session, complaining about the cold.

Without thinking, I picked her up and held her over the oil burner used to heat the office. I'm still not sure exactly what happened, but it was apparent that all the "sparks" weren't coming from the stove! Somehow I think she felt the sparks between us as strongly as I did.

Well, our paths didn't cross again for nearly 50 years, but neither of us forgot the other. We met again a few years ago, became reacquainted and then married.

The old spark is still there, I'm happy to say, and it warms us through the coldest winters Iowa can dish out. *—L.J. Lindemann, McGregor, Iowa*

They Found Hometown Happiness

IN 1945, a high school friend and I left the Midwest to go to work for the government in Washington, D.C. I got a job as a stenographer for the Chemical Warfare Service.

My friend and I loved seeing firsthand all the famous buildings and monuments we had only seen in books, but it sure was a long way from home in East Peoria, Illinois. I was 20 years old and homesick.

We lived in a rooming house which was right near the White House. One day in June I happened to look out our window and saw a handsome soldier moving in.

Later, when taking my mail from the stack that the postman always delivered inside the front door, I noticed some letters addressed to this young man, and they were from my home state! The postmark said "Table Grove, Illinois", which was only 15 miles from my hometown!

You can bet that when the opportunity arose, I introduced myself. After he had secured permission from our strict landlady, we began dating.

When Bob was discharged from the service and returned home, I, too, went home.

We were married on April 20, 1946. We still marvel that we met in Washington, D.C., when we were almost neighbors back home!

—*Erma Walters, Peoria, Illinois*

She Was 'Collared' by Cagey Sailor

I WAS IN high school in Lynn, Massachusetts in 1918. Armistice had been declared, and the servicemen were starting to come home.

One Sunday afternoon I was visiting my cousins. A young sailor, just back from the service, was at their home visiting as well.

We all had a pleasant afternoon, but the sailor soon had to leave. When he got up to go, he took his jacket, came over to me and asked if I would smooth down his sailor collar as he put the jacket on. I stood behind him but he said, "No, you have to stand in front of me and reach under my arms."

Poor naive girl that I was, I did as I was told. As I reached under his arms to smooth the corners of his collar, he kissed me.

Much later, his family told me he went home that day and told his grandmother he'd met the girl he was going to marry.

We did get married in October of 1922, and had a lovely send-off in our "new" Ford roadster. My sailor had purchased a Ford chassis for $15, and he and his chum finished building the car on the morning of our wedding day.

We drove that car to Maine for our honeymoon. It had big brass lamps and curtains with isinglass panels. We were the first in our crowd to have our own car—we thought we were really something special!

—*M.S. Hubbard, Groveland, Florida*

She Went 'Out on a Limb' for Love

IN THE FALL of 1932, I went to live with my aunt in Boulder County, Colorado. It was a pretty, wooded area, with Boulder Creek running through it.

One evening my aunt called me outside because the boy next door was up in a walnut tree shaking down nuts. She asked him to climb up the tree on our side of the fence so we could harvest some, too. My aunt introduced me to him while he was still in the tree.

All this time later, my husband loves to tell folks that I once found a nut up in a tree! I've been "nutty" about him ever since.

—*Sylvia Manchester, Boulder, Colorado*

Ewing Galloway

They Met by Mail

I WAS 18 years old in 1942, living in Oregon and doing my part for the war effort by writing letters to the boys I knew who were serving our country.

One of my pen pals was my cousin from Colorado. He wrote to tell me he'd shown my picture to his buddy, who now wanted to write me, too. I wrote my cousin and said okay.

In August 1942, I received my first letter from my cousin's buddy, a farm boy from Minnesota. That began a correspondence that lasted for 3 years.

In August of 1945, I agreed to take a trip with my 80-year-old grandfather back to his childhood home in Minnesota to visit his relatives.

The morning we boarded the train, I received a letter from the Minnesota Army buddy saying he was coming home soon and if I wanted to continue writing, I should send letters to his home at Windom, Minnesota.

Grandpa and I visited many places in Minnesota, and the last place was Redwood Falls, 45 miles from Windom. I called the buddy from there and he came to Redwood Falls, where we met in person for the first time in the home of my great-aunt. She and I were knitting when he arrived.

It didn't take us very long to decide we wanted to spend the rest of our lives together.

Grandpa and I returned home and I began making plans to be married. We were married in Oregon on October 22, 1945.

—Lula Leverenz
Windom, Minnesota

Their Love Was Sweet as Pie

ONE OF MY favorite forms of entertainment during my school days was the good old pie supper.

We girls would bake pies and bring them to the supper in decorated boxes. Then we'd try to get the goodies to the display table without the boys knowing whose pie was whose!

The pies were auctioned off by number, and later, the girl who'd baked the pie would share it with the successful bidder.

One evening I recall, a handsome young man still in high school was trying to bid. But with only $2 to spend, he was outbid on all the pies.

Another young man who had a good job at the nearby Navy installation purchased several pies. After the auction was over, he gave a few of his numbers to the men who didn't have any. One of his numbers happened to be mine.

Well, that handsome young man with only $2 in his pocket enjoyed some black raspberry pie with me that night. And he later became my husband.

We just celebrated 49 years together, and black raspberry is still his favorite pie!
                                        —*Mrs. Merle Lewis, Springville, Indiana*

How to Catch a Husband

MY WIFE "trapped" me back in school during the '30s. But then, she was pretty good at trapping...

All the kids carried lunches to school then, and we kept ours in our lockers. One day I went into the locker area to get my lunch and saw this pretty little girl standing there, almost in tears over something in her locker.

I went over to see if I could help her. The problem was, she had caught a mouse in a trap in her locker. It seems the pesky rodent had been helping itself to her lunches for some time, so she decided to put a stop to it.

She'd set the trap, caught the mouse, and now she couldn't bring herself to dispose of the critter!

Of course, this knight in shining armor was all too happy to rescue her from that dreadful task. We started dating soon afterward, and were married a few years later. When she caught that mouse, she caught my attention... and has held it ever since!
                                        —*Ralph Wells, Pittsburgh, Pennsylvania*

Color Him Curious

MY WIFE and I met at a single's club dance in Long Beach, California.

She was wearing a powder blue dress that matched her beautiful blue eyes. I was absolutely struck by those eyes, and we danced away the evening.

After the dance, I asked my blue-eyed beauty if she'd care to join me the next morning for a Sunday breakfast the club was hosting. She agreed.

When I picked her up the following morning, she was wearing a lovely green dress...that matched her beautiful *green* eyes. How could her eyes change color overnight? This had me curious! I later learned that she wore contact lenses and had a blue pair, a green pair and a clear pair.

We were married a year after we enjoyed our first dance together, but I've always said that she snared me with her beautiful eyes...blue, green or whatever color they were! —*Byron Reid, San Juan Capistrano, California*

The Ties That Bind

MY WIFE "roped me" but good!

The first time I saw her, she was turning a jump rope for her little sisters. I was supposed to be a big macho man, but I wanted to meet her so badly that I asked if I could turn one end of that jump rope for her! She was shy at first, but soon agreed.

So here I was, a teenage guy, turning a jump rope with a bunch of girls! I didn't mind it then, and I've never regretted it since.

In the decades that followed, our lives have turned richer with each passing year. If that's being "roped", I don't mind it one bit! —*Don West*
Myrtle Beach, South Carolina

They Met Once More

BACK IN 1927, a baby boy was born on a farm in Wisconsin. Twenty-eight days later, the neighboring farm welcomed a little girl into the world.

It was common custom in the area for the farm wives to gather at neighbors' homes to help with quilting, canning or whatever job needed doing.

Whenever the two families got together on such occasions, both mothers would put their babies to sleep in the same crib.

One year later, the parents of that baby boy moved to the city and the two families lost touch.

Sixteen years later, the two babies, now grown, met at a wedding. After exchanging names, they realized they'd been neighbors years before!

Letters traveled from city to country and back again. He proposed; she accepted.

As you've probably guessed, I was that little girl, and the boy, my husband. Together we've celebrated dozens of anniversaries.

—*Mrs. George Brzozowski, West Allis, Wisconsin*

*H*ard work was a way of life in the good old days—
and for many people back then, the work didn't
stop just because it happened to be someone's wedding day or
honeymoon!

Just as they normally did week in and week out, the newly-
weds in these photos did some backbreaking chores on their special days. But then, that shouldn't be very surprising...good
spouses always work well together!

WEDDING WRING. There was no escaping the drudgery of doing
the laundry for this young newly wedded couple. Mrs. Paul Oetz-
man of Sauk City, Wisconsin shared this laundry-day photograph of
her parents, which was taken during their honeymoon back in 1925.

BUILT WITH LOVE. Mr. and Mrs. N.O. Barkdoll, now of Sun City, Arizona, looked great at their evening wedding ceremony—even though they'd spent their entire wedding day working side by side, trying to get the roof on their new house (at right). The day was so hot they succeeded in roofing only half of it—but finished later.

She Found Her Fortune

IN 1939, when I was 17, a fortune teller told me I'd someday meet a tall dark-haired man, fall hard for him at first sight, get married and have five sons. I found that prediction pretty funny at the time.

In the spring of '40, a new family moved into our neighborhood. Through my brother, I met one of the sons of this family, and he happened to be tall and dark. He asked me to a dance, and although he didn't interest me very much, I consented to go.

My date's older brother happened to go to that dance, too, and after some time he asked me for a dance.

Before the dance was over, I knew he was the one for me. He was tall, dark and the most exciting person I'd ever met! I think he fell just as hard for me as I did for him, because 3 weeks later, we were married!

And, yes, we did have five sons!

—*Mrs. Forrest Miller*
Gibbon, Nebraska

She Was Head Over Heels in Love

YOU MIGHT SAY I fell for Bob in a big way.

In 1965, I was a teacher at a junior high school in Virginia Beach, Virginia. Bob was stationed on an amphibious command ship at the nearby Norfolk Navy base. A friend of mine from school knew some officers on this ship, and invited me to have dinner at the ship one evening.

After a tour of the ship, we retired to the wardroom to eat. I was all eyes, dazzled by the uniforms, the regalia and the pomp and circumstance of it all. We were halfway through the salad when Bob joined us.

All through dinner, his green eyes and raucous sense of humor captivated me. More than once I thought, "I wonder what it would be like to be married to him? He's a little too stocky for my taste, but he's certainly intriguing."

Years later, he told me that he was thinking the same sorts of things. "I wonder what it would be like to be married to her? She's a little too skinny, but she has the most gorgeous blue eyes." Love at first sight? I think so.

Dessert came, and with it my disappointment that dinner was almost over and I had not yet made a connection with this man.

As we concluded our visit, I walked out of the wardroom and onto the gangway steps. I lost my footing and fell down the equivalent of three flights of stairs toward the dock below.

Fortunately, Bob had gone ahead and caught me as I tumbled awkwardly down the stairs. He picked me up, made sure that I was okay and said, through my embarrassed giggles, "I'll call you tomorrow."

So when people ask me how Bob and I met, I can honestly say, "I fell for him!"
— *Margaret Ann Maricle, Los Osos, California*

Coffee Made Romance Perk

DURING THE '30s, I worked as a telephone operator for Western Union in Miami, Florida. I was assigned to the all-night shift, from 11 p.m. until 7 a.m.

I had a hard time staying awake, and once when I was especially sleepy, I called the night delivery manager to have one of our messengers bring me some coffee from the nearby cafe. (In those days there were no vending machines or cafeterias.)

The messenger who brought my coffee stayed and chatted awhile, then refused to let me pay for the coffee.

He continued to bring me coffee each night between his deliveries for Western Union and, you guessed it, he became my boyfriend and later my husband.

We were married in 1941 and raised three wonderful children. That simple cup of coffee really started something "perking"!
— *Elizabeth Killen, West Palm Beach, Florida*

They Took 'Crash Course' in Romance

SOME PEOPLE enjoy memories of meeting their future spouses by accident. Well, if anyone ever "met by accident", it was my husband and me!

Driving home from work one night, I was involved in a traffic accident. I was sitting in my car when the police and ambulance arrived.

The ambulance attendant did his best to console me, and insisted that I sit still even though I wished to get out and survey the damage. Though we didn't know it at the time, my future husband and I were having our first argument!

I was taken to an emergency room for minor treatment. Later, that amiable ambulance attendant phoned the hospital to see if I needed a ride home.

The following week, on our first date, I still had two very black eyes. But he must have seen something in those eyes, because 9 months later, we were married!
— *Cindy McCabe, Corona, California*

This Couple Met Under the Sea

LOCKED IN LOVE. Paul and Sylvia Lock were married in Valhalla, New York in 1946, after they'd become acquainted on a tour of a Navy submarine!

I MET my spouse under water …in a submarine!

It was October 1945, and I was visiting my cousin Ann in Staten Island. She asked if I would like to tour some submarines, which were berthed nearby and open to the public.

I certainly did! Ever since I'd studied about subs in grammar school science class, these ships had fascinated me.

Approaching the pier, we saw eight subs. We headed for the first, then changed our minds. We passed up the second. Then, for some reason, we were magnetically drawn to the third…maybe it was its name, *Cutlass*.

I descended the ladder and walked into the forward torpedo room, and listened to a sailor explaining a few things about operation of the sub. I continued to the engine room, and began conversing with a sailor.

Before I knew it, the room was full of sailors, all laughing and joking with me. At that moment, in walked sailor Paul Lock, whose duty was to see that visitors moved along through the ship.

He looked me straight in the eye and said, "I'll show you through the boat."

At that moment, my heart flipped! He was exceptionally handsome, and looking into his twinkling eyes, I could see he was the only lamb among a shipful of wolves.

As he gave me my tour, I didn't hear a word he said…I just stared at him. When he helped me out of the sub at the end of my tour, we made plans to meet later that evening.

We were engaged January 14, 1946, and married in June of that year. Our "underwater romance" has been bubbling right along ever since.

—*Sylvia Lock, Ellsworth, Maine*

She Was One Lucky Girl

I LIVED in a small town in northwest Georgia. In fall of 1944, a good friend who was in the Navy managed to come home on leave and he asked me for a date.

There weren't many choices for entertainment. Once you'd seen both movies playing in town you could see them again. Or, on this particular weekend, you could go to the county fair that was being held on the outskirts of town. My date and I went to the fair.

And so did nearly everyone else in the county! The ticket lines for every ride were long and slow.

Being smart, my date put me in line to wait to ride the Ferris wheel while he stood in another line to buy tickets. As I was standing there, a little boy tugged at my elbow and asked, "Are you with that Navy fellow?" When I told him yes, he said, "Boy, are you lucky!"

I stood in that line just long enough to realize that, yes, I *was* lucky to be with that Navy fellow. And to this day, I still think so!

—*Kathryn Mason, Pensacola, Florida*

She Was His 'Special Delivery'

BACK IN 1925, when I lived in Winslow, Arkansas, the cutest little girl delivered our mail on horseback. I often tried to talk to her, but she would just give her horse a kick and dash off down the road.

During the summer of 1926, I got a job driving a bus between Winslow and Fayetteville. One Saturday, who should get on my bus but that little mail carrier!

It was raining by the time we reached Winslow, so I offered her a ride right to her house. Before she got off we made a date to go walking the next day.

Well, Mary and I dated for about 6 months, then one Saturday while I was walking her home I turned to her and said, "Let's get married."

"All right," she answered.

The following week we went to the county seat to buy a marriage license. When the clerk asked when we wanted to be married, he was surprised when we said, "Today".

"You must not be superstitious," he said. "Today's Friday the 13th, you know!" I told him to go ahead and issue the license anyway, because I knew that we probably wouldn't have the money to come back another day.

That day turned out to be the luckiest day of my life...I finally had my cute little mail carrier. And she's delivered me nothing but happiness!

—*Raymond Jones, Yakima, Washington*

Their Love Took Wing

NOT MANY COUPLES can say their marriage was the result of an airplane crash. But my husband and I can.

Back in 1951, a young man who roomed at my family's house owned a small plane. One day he was going to give someone a ride, but the plane failed to gain altitude on takeoff and crashed in a farm field.

We were notified of the accident, and the pilot asked me to contact a friend of his and relay the news.

I called that friend, and he asked if our family was going to go visit him in the hospital. When I said we were, he asked if he could ride along. I said yes, and started our 2-year courtship which ended with a very pretty church wedding on October 17, 1953.

After the reception, we drove to Casper, Wyoming, where we had reservations at a ranch to go deer hunting. On arrival, we learned our accommodations were in a sheep wagon. A sheep wagon resembles a covered wagon, only with a metal covering instead of cloth as the pioneers used.

Our courtship and honeymoon were most unusual, but despite it all, our love has been deep and lasting.

—*Mrs. William McCollum*
St. Charles, Missouri

One Look Led to Love

WHEN I WAS 6 years old, I attended a church dinner with my parents. Four boys, age 10, entertained us with some great quartet singing.

One boy in particular dazzled me. He had black hair and deep dark eyes, and he was singing his heart out. I was *sure* his songs were meant just for me!

I had such a crush on him, I didn't want to go home with Mother and Dad when they left. I wanted to stay and hear that boy as long as I could!

I thought about the cute little boy off and on through the years, smiling at the thought of how smitten I was at such a tender age. I didn't even know his name.

When I was 16, I met another young man who stole my heart the first time he smiled at me. He also had thick black hair and black flashing eyes.

We had been married over a year when I happened to open a photo album at his mother's house. On the first page was a picture of the quartet that sang at our church years ago...and on the end was my little sweetheart!

I asked my mother-in-law who that little boy was and she started laughing. She said, "You should know, you married him!" —Margie Frazier
Frankston, Texas

They Were Streetcar Sweethearts

I MOVED to Dallas in 1939 to attend beauty school. I lived with my older sister, Delila. Neither of us had a car, so the streetcar was our only means of transportation.

While riding the streetcar one night, Delila said to me, "Did you notice the driver keeps looking at you?"

I hadn't, but after that, I paid more attention to the operator. I saw him every morning and afternoon on that streetcar, and one day he introduced himself as George Sheehan.

"I'm Myrtle," I said, not volunteering my last name.

Soon my sister and I moved, which meant I'd take another streetcar line to school. The day we moved I rode home with George as usual. As I got off I told him that I enjoyed riding his car, but I was moving and wouldn't be seeing him anymore. He asked the name of the street I'd be moving to, and I told him.

A few weeks later I stepped on the streetcar, and who do you suppose was the operator? George Sheehan, at your service!

After some months, I graduated from beauty school and took a job in downtown Dallas. I had to use yet another streetcar to get to work.

One night I got on the streetcar to go home, and you can guess who the driver was! George had found me again, but this time he wouldn't let me go.

When I was one block from my stop, I gave the signal that I'd be getting off, but the door wouldn't open. I tried the next stop, and still the door wouldn't open.

I was too timid, shy and embarrassed to complain, and I was getting too far from home to walk. After the last passenger got off, George finally turned to me with a smile. "Now, I'll let you off if you'll tell me your last name and where you live."

That was the beginning of our courtship, and we spent most of it riding on the streetcar together. George was supporting his parents on 49¢ an hour, and any time off was lost pay.

My George proposed on that streetcar one rainy night in November of 1940. That Christmas he gave me a ring, and we were married on June 1, 1941. You might say I rode the rails to romance!

—Myrtle Sheehan
Powderly, Texas

Storekeeper's Son Was Man with a Plan

THE YEAR was 1935, and my future husband had been put in charge of running his family's small-town grocery store.

I was a senior in high school that year, and one day this grocer's son saw me walk past the store. He decided we had to meet, so he found a mutual friend who would introduce us. The next Saturday, they came out to visit at my home in the country, and I found that storekeeper's son to be quite charming.

I don't think his father ever knew he had to lock up the store on a busy Saturday morning in order to make that trip to meet me!

—Dorothy Armintrout, Allegan, Michigan

She Got Her 'Just Desserts'

ONE EVENING during my junior year in college, my sorority invited one of the fraternities over for coffee and some sweets. This "dessert" was meant to be a way of getting acquainted, and it worked. A handsome senior asked me out for a date!

We dated until he graduated and left school for his hometown. I, of course, still had another year of college to go.

I really cared about him, but now we were over 400 miles apart. One day I wondered out loud to my friend how I could make this relationship continue. She thought a little bit and advised me to send him a note.

Since I wanted my note to get his attention, I sent him the following "invitation":

Miss Shirley Ann Young
Requests the Pleasure
Of Receiving a Letter
From
Mr. Anthony M. Marzullo
At His Earliest Convenience!

To make a long story short, I received a letter *and* a proposal. I guess I got his attention...and we've been paying attention to one another for over 35 years! —*Shirley Marzullo, Cos Cob, Connecticut*

COURTIN' COUPE. John and Dorothy Galley posed in front of this handsome Oldsmobile during the summer of 1940. That great old car squired them through their courtship in New Jersey. Many exciting trips to Atlantic City later, and the happy couple was married.

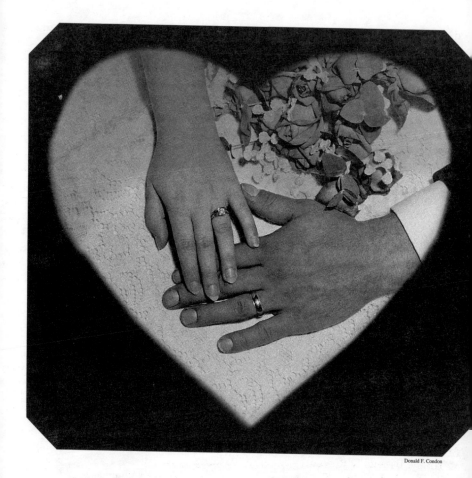

A Ring Was Just the Thing

AS A 16-YEAR-OLD-GIRL, my mother attended a small country church in Pennsylvania. Most everyone knew each other.

One Sunday before church services began, my mother was sitting in the front row and turned around to look at the congregation. Her eyes met those of a young man she'd never met. In that brief moment, a warm smile and a wink from him was all it took to cause my mother to believe in love at first sight!

She later told me her first thought was, "This is the man I'm going to marry!"

That day she didn't linger in church, but quickly made her way out, hoping to see him. Once again their eyes met, and another encouraging smile from him gave her the courage to say hello. From there the relationship blossomed.

On their way to the movies one evening, they paused at the window of a jewelry store to look at a display of rings. With a little prompting from him, she pointed out one she thought was pretty. Then they continued on to the movie.

Shortly after being seated, my dad told my mom he'd be right back. When he returned, the lights were out and the movie had started. He sat down, took her hand and slipped that ring on her finger.

A couple of warm smiles and a little wink in church was how it all began for my parents over 40 years ago. —*Vickie Sluga, Randolph, New York*

He's Getting Even!

MY HUSBAND, Ernest, and I met when he was 10 and I was 8. Ernest liked me and, as little boys so often do to show their affection, he made himself an utter nuisance!

Ernest would follow me around all day and pull my hair. In return, I would beat him up. Then Ernest would run home crying, saying, "I'm gonna get my big sister to beat *you* up!" I never saw his sister.

Eight years later, Ernest and I happened to meet and he asked me out to the county fair. I accepted. As time went by, we dated more often. We were eventually married.

Today, friends who recall our early "battling" years think it's funny that we're married. To this, Ernest remarks, "I'm with her now just to get even!"

If this is "getting even", I hope it goes on forever! —*Ina Reed*
Whittier, California

Separator Brought Them Together

THE SUMMER after my first year of college, my cousin asked me to stay at her farm for a couple of weeks to help out after her baby was born.

My first job was to wash the cream separator. Being a city girl, I'd never actually done this chore myself, but I had watched my grandmother do it once, so I thought it was no big deal. I went to take that machine apart, and, *zoom*, about 30 discs flew out of it, rolling every which way onto the porch and lawn!

A younger brother of my cousin's husband had come over to help out on the farm, too, and he saw my predicament.

"Need some help?" he asked.

I was so embarrassed, but I said that I could manage. After I'd washed the parts, I tried to reassemble them.

"Wait a minute," he said. "You're putting it together wrong. Each disc is numbered and needs to be put back in rotation."

By the time he and I put that cream separator back together, we had become nicely acquainted. Four years later, that helpful boy and I were married...and to think a "separator" once brought us together.

—*Mrs. Rudy Busacker, Long Prairie, Minnesota*

Decades Later, the Meter's Still Ticking!

IN 1955, I was a single young policeman living at home and working the 3-to-11 p.m. shift. My first 2 hours were usually spent walking a beat and checking parking meters.

One afternoon I met several young ladies just as they were returning to their car. Time was expired on the meter, but the driver quickly dropped a nickel in the slot. We joked about the ticket I said I was going to give them, and they went on their way.

A few days later I had the night off. My date and I were at the local drive-in. Parked right next to us was the driver of the "ticketed car". I asked her for a date and she said yes. Three weeks later I gave her a diamond, and she again said yes.

We've had dozens of wonderful years together and I still tease her by saying: "Your parking ticket only cost you a nickel, but look what it's cost me over all these years!"

—*Dana Morse, Goshen, Indiana*

When Country Met City

I MET FOLKS from all over the country when I left my rural home to attend Bible college. One day as I walked to class, I saw two young men who talked so strangely I could hardly understand them. One was from Pittsburgh and the other from Brooklyn. Because of their accents, I dismissed them as "city toughs" and knew they weren't my kind.

I worked on campus during the summer, and so did the boy from Brooklyn. I eventually got to know him, and he didn't seem so bad after all. He did yard work all day long in the summer heat, and one day he told me he was having trouble staying awake for our school's youth conferences held in the evenings.

I usually attended those conferences with another girl, and I assured this boy that we'd be happy to accept the challenge of keeping him awake. We'd sit on each side of him and give him a poke in the ribs when he fell asleep!

The following evening my girlfriend made other plans and left me alone at the conference with my new friend. For the remainder of the summer he and I attended meetings together, hiked and just enjoyed each other's company.

You know, that accent wasn't bad after all...and this "city tough" turned out to be caring, sensitive and a real gentleman. Over 50 years later, we're still going strong! —*Evelyn Bollback, Omaha, Nebraska*

Her Redhead Rode the Rumble Seat

I HAD BEEN walking a mile each day to high school back in 1939, but sometimes a senior named Faith would stop to give underclassmen like me a lift.

Faith was the proud owner of a 1937 Plymouth coupe with a rumble seat, and one autumn day when she stopped to pick me up, she had an unfamiliar redheaded boy sitting in the rumble seat. I hopped in front with Faith.

"Who's the redhead?" I asked.

She made a face and said, "He's my younger brother."

I told her I thought he was cute.

"Ugh!" she cried. "If he ever kisses you, let me know!" (She seemed to find that thought infinitely amusing.)

Eventually, he did kiss me, and I ended up marrying that redheaded boy. Our life together has been both a long one and a happy one, and we're often grateful for the day his sister stopped to give me a ride—and that he happened to be tagging along in that rumble seat! —*Jane Wyman*
Newton, Massachusetts

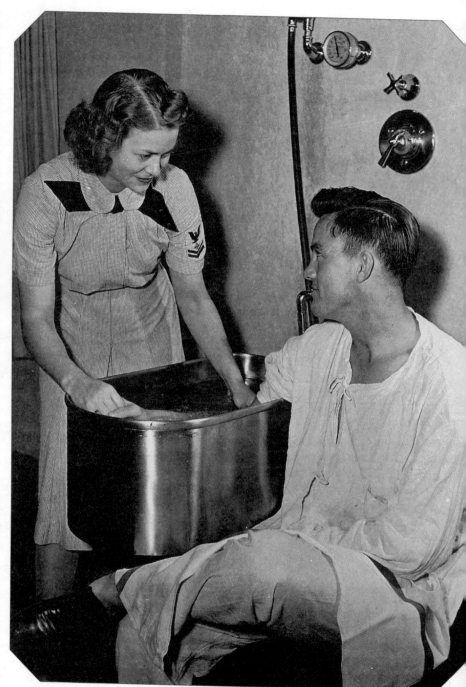

He Married an Angel!

THE WAR in Europe was winding down. It was 1945, and slowly our boys were returning home to the loved ones they'd left behind.

I was a student nurse working the midnight-to-8 a.m. shift at a New York hospital, and I provided care for some of those boys.

One evening the supervisor was giving me a patient-by-patient report. When she came to the last one she said, "The young soldier in room 302 came in without any identification—his dog tags were lost. He won't live till morning."

Well, he did live till morning…and many mornings after that. I know, because he's now my husband!

He still likes to tell me that when he came to that night and saw me standing there in my crisp white uniform and cap, he thought he'd died and saw an angel. I'm not sure that's true, but I still like to believe it!

—Ada Metzing, Walden, New York

A Battery-Charged Romance Sparked Their Love

IT WAS SUMMER of 1947 and I'd just graduated from high school. I took a job and had bought myself a new portable radio with some of the money I'd made, and decided to try it out at the beach. A few of my girlfriends from school went along.

We'd no sooner spread our blanket on the sand at Belmar Beach, New Jersey, when we realized we didn't have a clue how to load the batteries into my radio. In those days, batteries were very large, and not nearly as common as they are today.

We noticed the same model radio sitting on an empty beach blanket near ours, so we decided to ask the owner for some help when he or she returned. Soon, a tall handsome blond fellow and two dark-haired friends came back to the blanket, and we wasted no time asking *them* how to go about loading the batteries.

This was the beginning of a friendship and then romance, not only for me and that blond fellow but for one of my girlfriends and another one of those three boys. I married that blond fellow 2 years later, and the other couple married, too! *—Ruth Gunderson, Bradley Beach, New Jersey*

Fate Was Great to This Couple

LUCKY PAIR. A series of fateful events brought Bill and Ruth Protz together during the war years.

DOES FATE bring people together? I don't know, but there's probably no other way to explain how my husband and I met. By all rights, we probably shouldn't even have laid eyes on one another.

It was 1944 in Milwaukee, Wisconsin. A group of my friends were working as hostesses at the "Navy Fathers' Dance", a weekly party held for servicemen. They'd asked me many times to attend but I'd always declined...until one Sunday in September.

Bill, meanwhile, had been a hospital corpsman stationed in Boston. He was readying for assignment to Florida when an unexplained change in orders sent him to Great Lakes Naval Training Center in Illinois. After he arrived, for some reason, he chose to visit Milwaukee on that September Sunday.

Bill went to the Navy Fathers' Dance and he pursued me all afternoon, but I wasn't interested. After some time, he left the dance to accompany one of his buddies back to the bus depot.

That soldier knew Bill's mind was still on "a certain girl at the dance", so he encouraged Bill to go back and try again. He did, and this time, his persistence paid off.

Bill and I were married the following June. Through the years, we've often wondered what made me attend the Navy Fathers' Dance on that particular day, why Bill was shipped to Illinois instead of Florida, and if that soldier remembers the day he "nudged" us together...forever.

—*Ruth Protz, Oshkosh, Wisconsin*

He Danced with a 'Knockout'

YOU COULD SAY my future bride really fell for me.

Back in 1932, I went to a dance at the town hall in Plainfield, Utah. Right away, I noticed a very attractive young lady who was a great dancer. I asked her for the next dance, and she agreed.

We ended up dancing together most of the evening. It was quite warm in the hall and the music got faster and faster. Soon a crowd formed a circle around us and she and I were the only ones dancing.

Suddenly, in the middle of the floor, she fainted dead away in my arms! I picked her up and carried her outside for some air, and she quickly recovered.

She went home with the woman who accompanied her to the dance, and I didn't see her again for 6 months.

When we finally did meet again, my dance partner certainly remembered me...and we were married less than a year after that.

We're still together all these years later, and we still enjoy an occasional dance...and recall with a laugh the time my wife "fell" for me.
—*L.W. Densmore, Bellows Falls, Vermont*

Slim Santa Made Her Merry

I TAUGHT at a little one-room schoolhouse in western South Dakota, and at Christmastime, all my students were *so* excited.

We were busy decorating, making gifts and practicing for our Christmas program, which was a big social event in our area. Folks from miles around would be attending!

I had one big problem, though...there was no one I knew who could play the part of Santa Claus.

A friend learned of my predicament and she told me about a nice young man on a nearby ranch who might be willing to help out.

When I met the man, I was pleased to hear he'd be happy to take the Santa job. But he was tall and thin, and I didn't know how he'd ever fill that Santa suit!

With a few pillows, a white beard and a jolly *Ho! Ho! Ho!*, he ended up making a fine Santa Claus.

Later, he became a fine husband...and we've been merry for 55 years!
—*Dorothy Herman, Sioux Falls, South Dakota*

For This Couple, the Parsonage Was the Place

IN OCTOBER 1940, my father accepted a call to be the minister at an impoverished church and he moved our family to the parsonage.

I was 13 years old and the youngest of seven children. All of us were expected to pitch in, teaching Sunday school, singing in the choir and being of service in whatever way we could.

Since the church needed fixing up, my father hired several young men to go to work on the building. One of those men caught my eye! He was so handsome, with his dark hair and blue eyes, and from then on, he was "the one".

Once Bob and I got acquainted, I began finding small gifts hidden in my coat pockets. And, suddenly, he became one of our most regular Sunday school attendants as well as a member of the choir.

Soon he left for World War II, and as he served, he prayed daily, as did I.

After the war, my prayers were answered ...we were engaged! We married 3 weeks later. It took some fast planning, a lot of help from the church members and a borrowed gown for me, but it was the greatest moment of my life.

—*Beatrice Whitehead*
Warrenton, Virginia

CUT THE CAKE! Bob and Beatrice Whitehead did the honors (far left) at their 1948 wedding. The couple met and dated through the early '40s, even though Bob would ship off to serve in World War II. Occasional furlough visits (left) were a treat. Today, Bob and Beatrice's love remains as strong as when they met and fell in love.

Operator Got This Trooper's Message

BACK IN 1948, I was a telephone operator at the old "cord switchboard" in Corning, New York. I worked the 5-to-11 evening shift with about 40 other operators.

One night a young New York state trooper placed a call to his station through my switchboard. He'd received a radio transmission to call for a message, and in those days of "one-way radio", the station could reach the patrol cars, but troopers had to go to the nearest phone to communicate with the station.

On this night, the police station's line was busy, so the trooper asked me if he could stay on the line and wait. I said yes, and since it was a slow night for me, I chatted with him for a time. He did his "detective work" and found out my name and where I lived.

At the end of my shift, I caught the bus and rode home. When I got off, was I surprised to see a black-and-white State Patrol car following me into the driveway!

We talked some more, made a date for the next night, and within a year, were married.

I've always been grateful that out of 40 operators, I was the one who happened to pick up this young trooper's call...and that two-way radios weren't invented yet!　　　　　　　　　　　　　　　—*Virginia Shaver, Avon, New York*

She Heard His Question

WHEN MY CHURCH installed hearing aids, I moved to a pew that was equipped with them, and sat down next to a handsome elderly gentleman.

When the sermon was finished, we discovered that the wires of our hearing aid receivers had become crossed. Getting those wires untangled started our first conversation.

The following Wednesday night at our church supper, he took a place in line next to me and paid for my meal. Later, he asked if he might take me to the Valentine banquet the next Thursday, and I was pleased to accept.

We met some of his friends at the party, but when he started to introduce me, memory failed him—he'd forgotten my name! He whispered to me, "If you'd let me change your name, I wouldn't have this problem."

I laughed at that, thinking it was a cute joke. I soon learned that this gentleman wasn't joking, however—because 5 months later we were married!

The wedding of a 92-year-old man and his 73-year-old bride made the first page of our local newspaper. Hearing aids or not, I sure heard him when he asked "the question".   —*Mrs. Gilbert Maloney, Aiken, South Carolina*

He Came to Her Rescue!

ON a wintry day in the 1930s, my father and I were riding in his 1928 Chevrolet. As we were about to cross some railroad tracks, the car stalled.

There we were, stuck on the tracks, when a handsome young man came along. He tinkered with the engine, but it just wouldn't go. In desperation, he hooked on a tow chain and pulled us off the tracks—and all the way home.

We invited the boy in for dinner, and he became my beau.

These days, when we tell that "rescue story" to our children, grandchildren and great-grandchildren, we conveniently fail to mention that only two trains per day used those tracks, and the next one wasn't due for hours!
—*Kathryn McGaughey, Denver, Colorado*

German Lessons Led to Romance

TO FURTHER my career as an export manager, I decided to take German lessons. I placed an ad for a German tutor, and a charming young lady named Violeta responded.

We agreed to meet every Thursday evening for lessons. Soon my lessons turned into Sunday matinees at a German theater on 86th Street in New York City, followed by dinner at a German restaurant. It was after one of these dinners in our favorite little German restaurant that I told Violeta I loved her and asked her to marry me.

Our 30th anniversary is coming up soon…and I still haven't mastered the German language! Violeta says that's my own fault for paying more attention to the teacher than my studies!   —*Emil Ilges*
Santa Barbara, California

She Fell for Her Fellow—
In Middle of the Fun House

THE LOCAL CHURCH YOUTH GROUP was going to Venice Pier, an amusement park in Southern California, and I was invited to go along.

The park was great until I tried out the fun house, which wasn't as fun as billed. I was trying to go through a rolling barrel when I fell and couldn't get up. No matter how often I tried, I just couldn't get my feet back under me.

I guess I'd still be rolling around in that barrel if it wasn't for the big handsome guy who came to my rescue.

He picked me up by the leather belt on my slacks and carried me out like a suitcase! Of course, we became friends that night.

We started dating and were later voted "Senior Sweethearts". We were married on graduation day in 1945.

What started in a fun house has been nothing but fun ever since!

—*Dorothy Fox, Meadview, Arizona*

They're Still Making Music!

MY HUSBAND and I met at the altar!

It was 1949 when a friend asked me to play the organ for her wedding. My future husband was a friend of the groom's and was asked to sing.

We met and rehearsed at the church, practicing our songs until we were all set for the big event.

On the day of the wedding, the old pump organ broke down. There was no organ music...no wedding march for the bride...nothing! I was so upset I cried during the whole ceremony. My future husband sang without accompaniment and tried to console me.

The bride's aunt later told people that I was so overcome with emotion I was unable to play! (But I did manage to "recover" enough to catch the bouquet at the reception!)

Sure enough, 2 months later, that sympathetic singer and I were engaged. We were married in April of 1950.

I'm still playing the organ and he's still singing, and we do so together as often as possible. —*Madeline Branen, Staten Island, New York*

A Real Romantic Entanglement

BACK IN 1935, I had a dog named "Sandy" who loved to play in the water. Every day we'd go for a walk in a meadow that had a brook running through it.

That meadow was surrounded by a barbed wire fence, and the only way to get into the meadow was to crawl through the fence.

One day as Sandy and I headed toward the meadow for our walk, I noticed a beautiful girl picking violets. As she picked, she tried to crawl under the fence—but she got entangled in the wire!

I was all too happy to come to her rescue, and just 3 months later, we were married!

Esther and I have come to each other's rescue in so many ways through the years...and I still can't help but laugh about the time she got "tangled up in love"! —*Paul Spiese, Santa Maria, California*

Common Tastes Led Them
To an Uncommon Meeting

AS A YOUNGSTER, I never liked the smell of onions, and I couldn't bring myself to eat them whether cooked or raw. This upset my mother who assured me that, "All men like onions". She was worried that I'd have a hard time cooking for a husband when I married.

As time went on, I took a job as a waitress. One day a young man walked into the restaurant and gave me his order: "Liver and onions...and hold the onions".

Here was the man for me!

He asked me to go dancing, and I accepted even though I couldn't dance. We fell in love and eventually married.

Over 4 decades later we love each other as much as ever...and still can do without the onions! —*Bernice Weber, Columbiana, Ohio*

More Memorable Reading! From... *Reminisce*

66